I Wear a Mask

Written by Dr. Kimberly Brayman
and Peter Borich

Illustrated by Dr. Kimberly Brayman

Copyright © 2021 by Dr. Kimberly Brayman

All rights reserved. No part of this publication may be reproduced, stored in a retrieval system, or transmitted in any form or by any means, electronic, mechanical, photocopying, recording, or otherwise, without written permission by the author.

For information regarding permission please write to:
Dr. Kimberly Brayman: info@KimberlyBraymanAuthor.com

For bulk and wholesale orders please email Dr. Kimberly Brayman: info@KimberlyBraymanAuthor.com

ISBN: 978-1-951688-38-7 (paperback)

Written and Illustrated by: Dr. Kimberly Brayman

First Edition

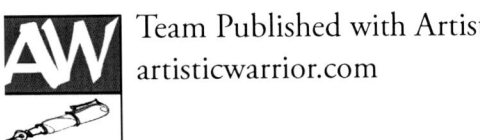

Team Published with Artistic Warrior
artisticwarrior.com

Dedicated to those who wear a mask,
in an effort to keep us all safe.

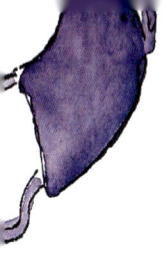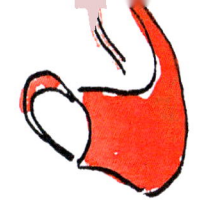

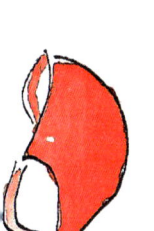

I did not want to, I did not ask,
But suddenly I wore a mask.
It felt so strange and so uncool,
To have to wear a mask at school.

"Lots of people wear masks each day,"
I heard my mama laugh and say.
"Let's pretend, let us see.
Let's imagine who we can be."

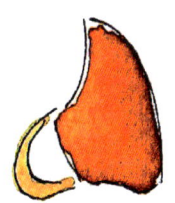

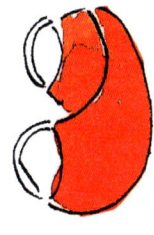

I wear a mask and I can be . . .
a pirate!

I am a pirate out at sea,
Brave and wild, and fancy free.
Hunting treasure is a pirate's life;
We laugh, we sing, we play with dice.

With sturdy boots and a hard hat, too,
and masks for certain jobs I do.
With wood and concrete, steel and glass,
I build it strong so it will last.

I chase a steer that bucks and whirls.
In the air, a lasso I twirl.
My horse is pinto, black and white,
We work all day and rest at night.

I wear a mask and I can be . . .
a nurse!

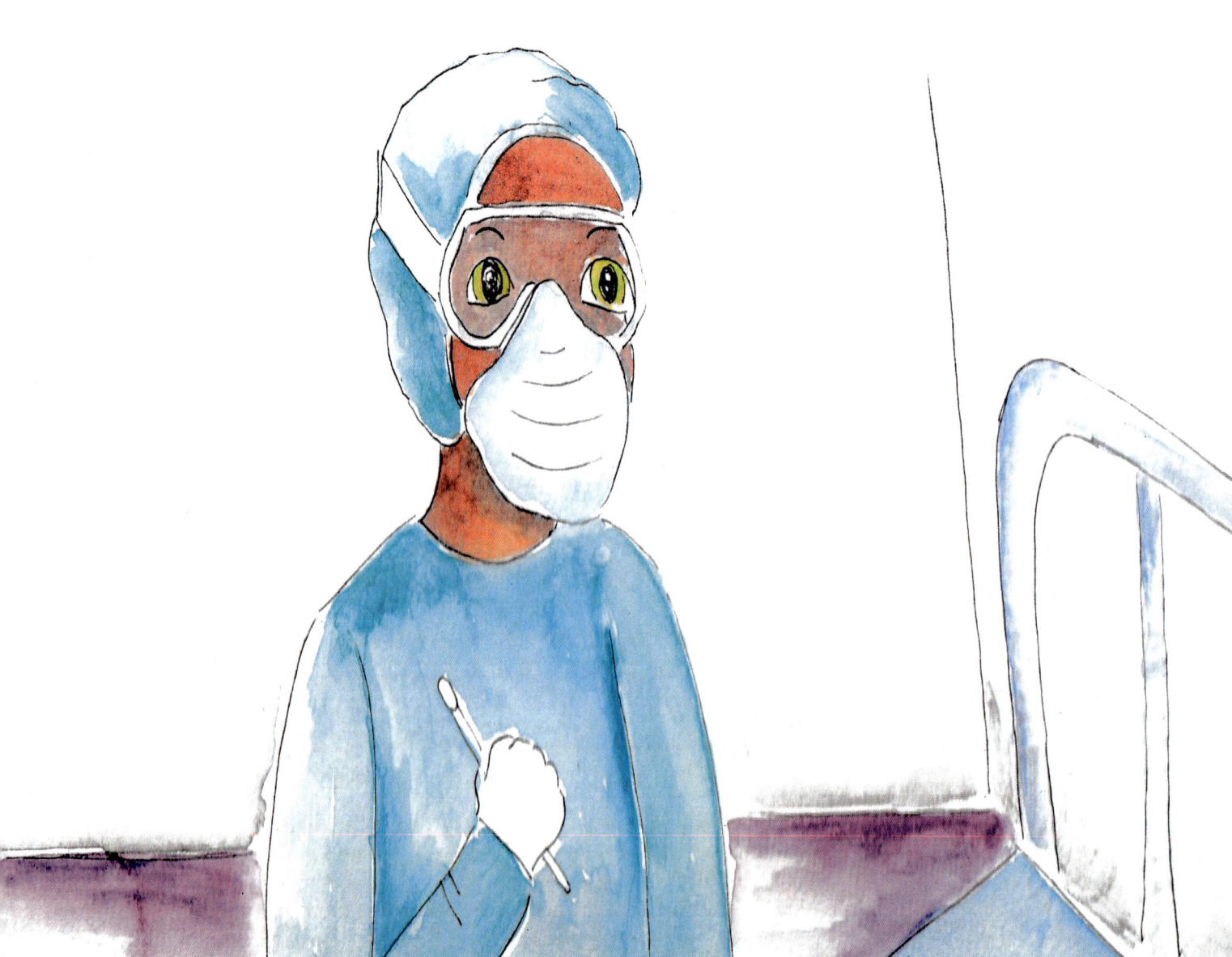

All day long I care for others,
mothers, fathers, sisters, brothers.
I try to help them feel their best,
Then send them home to get some rest.

I wear a mask and I can be . . .
an artist!

Orange, yellow, pink, and blue,
colors for me and colors for you.
My happy place is making art,
It brings me joy and fills my heart.

I wear a mask and I can be . . .
a dentist!

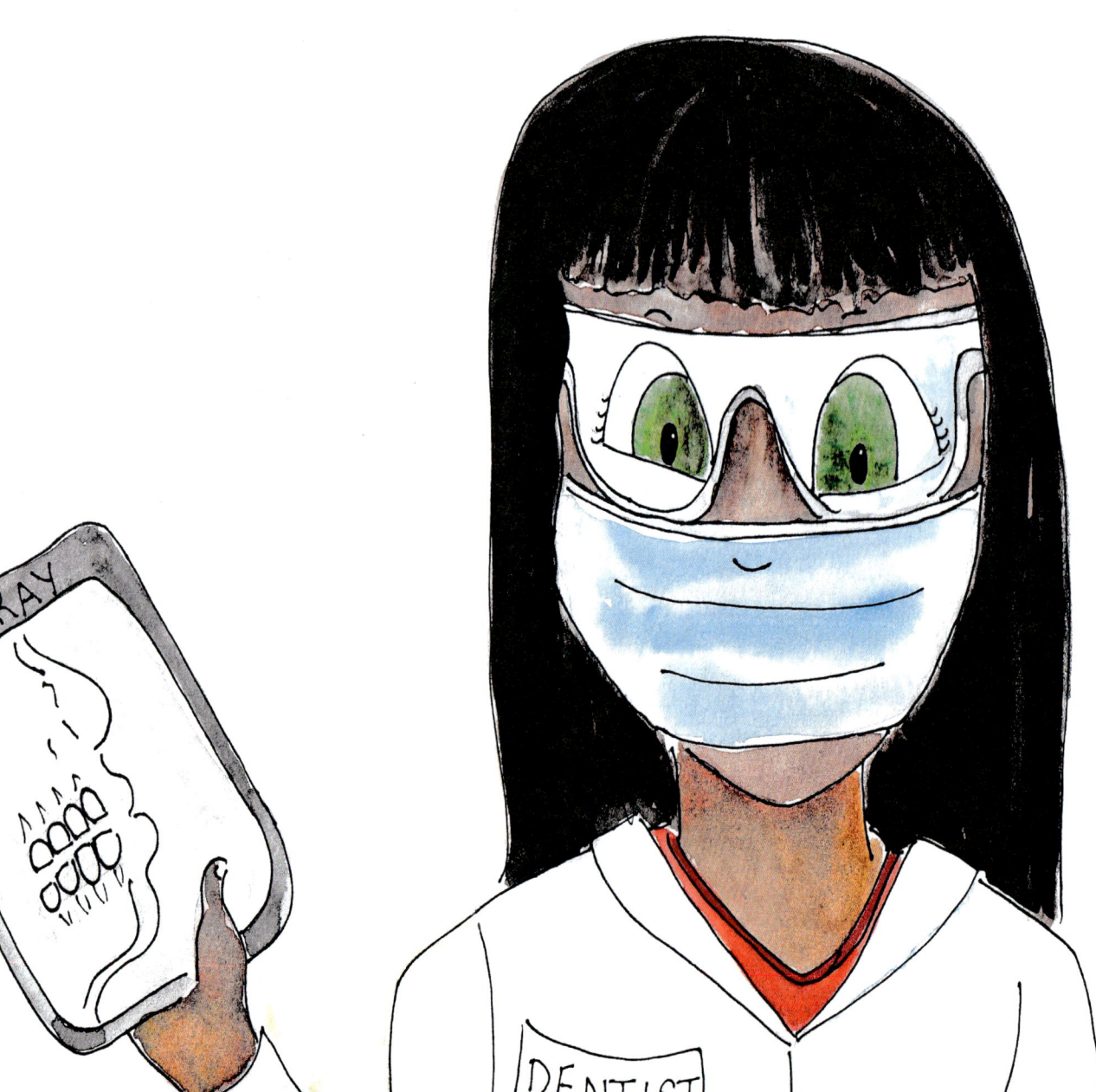

I want your teeth to shine so bright,
A gleaming smile of pearly white.
X-rays, cleaning, I do it all,
For the big and for the small.

I have a baseball glove and bat,
And wear my favorite baseball cap.
What else we wear, you might well ask.
When on the bench we wear our masks.

I wear a mask and I can be . . .
a dog trainer!

I train all kinds of dogs each day,
with time for work and time for play.
Their owners come to take a class.
To keep us safe we wear our masks.

I wear a mask and I can be . . .
a firefighter!

I fight fires; I am brave,
Forests and houses are ablaze.
The flames are hot, the smoke dark gray;
We fight the flames and save the day.

My coffee shop has charm and grace
with trinkets, books, and bakery case.
Espresso, mocha, hot chocolate too,
I'm here to make them all for you.

I wear a mask and I can be . . . anyone I want to be!

Masks are worn by everyone,
To imagine all of them is fun.
So, when you wear your mask, let's see,
who is it that you can be!

Author and Illustrator Dr. Kimberly Brayman

After decades of working in health care, Dr. Kimberly Brayman was inspired to build confidence, normalize struggle, inspire hope, and delight adults and children alike through her storytelling.

She believes stories build empathy and empower the listener to find their own self-reliance and strength. The power of supportive relationships is a strong theme in her stories. When a child knows deep in their heart that they are loved and accepted, just the way they are, they have a chance to blossom.

Dr. Brayman enjoyed creating the whimsical watercolor illustrations in this book. "Art is the playground for my inner child."

As of 2021, Dr. Brayman is a registered psychologist (registration #2464) in British Columbia, Canada. She has also been a registered psychologist in Colorado, USA.

Written with Peter Borich

Peter's background is as a teacher and lecturer in the education world, and as a copywriter and wordsmith in the business world.

He was thrilled to lend a musical ear and any subsequent word-smithing to the singsong rhythms of a children's book.

Other Illustrated Children's Books by Dr. Kimberly Brayman

Artsy Alphabet
Count With Me!
Nana Loves You More
Blueberries
I Want to Be
We Are Different and the Same
Will You Be My Friend?
The Magical Fisherman

Available on Amazon

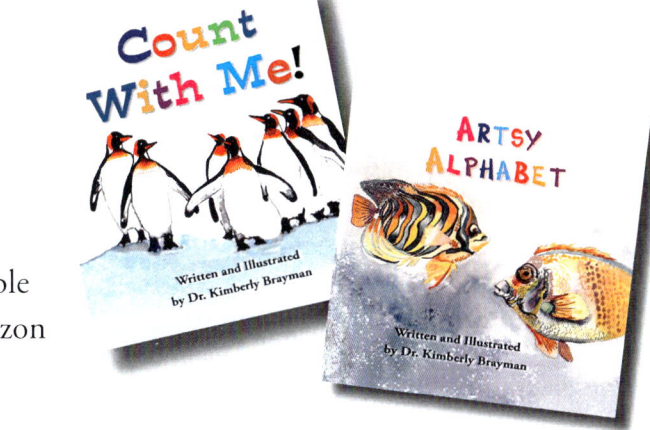

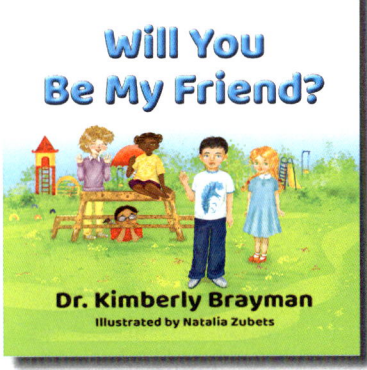
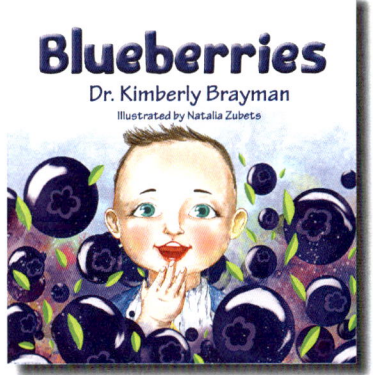

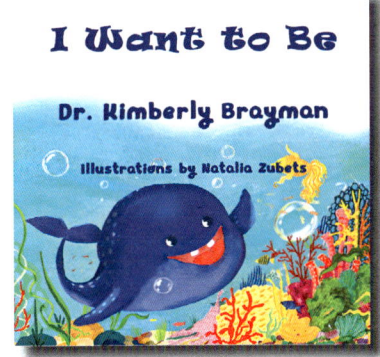
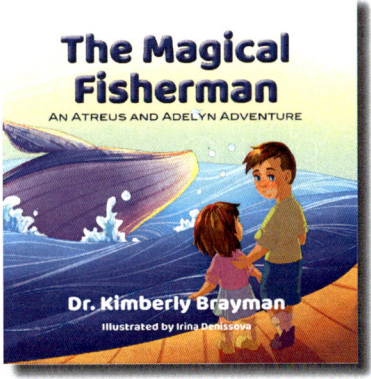
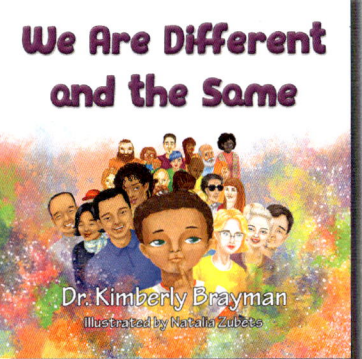

Chapter Books for Young Readers
Marshmallow the Magic Cat Adventures

Avry's Magical Cat: A Marshmallow the Magic Cat Adventure
Avry adopts a cat from the animal shelter and discovers he is magical like her Nana. She lives close to nature and has a magical view of the world.

A Troll in the Woods: A Marshmallow the Magic Cat Adventure
A true quest that shows courage and fear can go hand in hand, and the power of friendship to inspire action.

Avry and Atreus Save Christmas: A Marshmallow the Magic Cat Adventure
A delightful Christmas tale to be read every holiday season. It's full of elves, ravens, and the capability inside all children to redeem themselves and be good.

Marshmallow Paints the Town: A Marshmallow the Magic Cat Adventure
A fun story that focuses on collaboration, self-responsibility, making mistakes and recovering.

Marshmallow Gets a Little Sister: A Marshmallow the Magic Cat Adventure
Avry brings home a stray kitten, which makes Marshmallow very unhappy. He does not want a little sister and he wants to get rid of her. Is there really enough love to go around?

A Trip to the Hot Springs: A Marshmallow the Magic Cat Adventure
Avry is struggling because the kids at school are teasing her. Marshmallow calls Nana who takes them on a vacation to the hot springs. They have several adventures and Avry learns to conquer her fear of tunnels and how to relax in a world that sometimes feels too big for her.

Visit the author's website at KimberlyBraymanAuthor.com for updates.

Older children love
the adventures of Marshmallow the Magic Cat

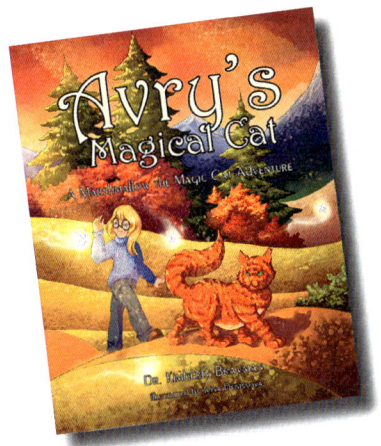  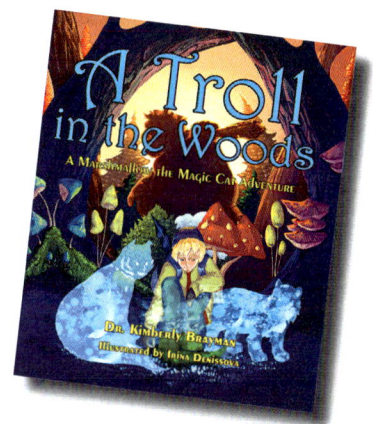

Get yours now on Amazon

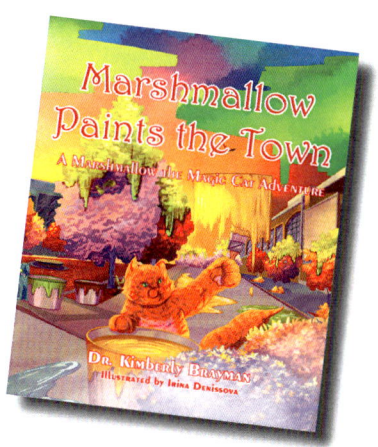 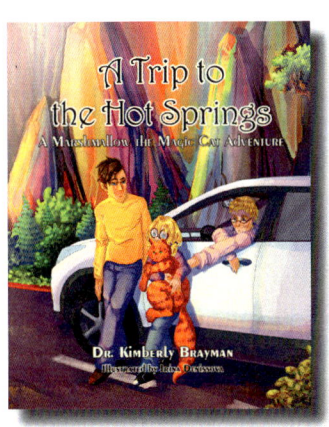 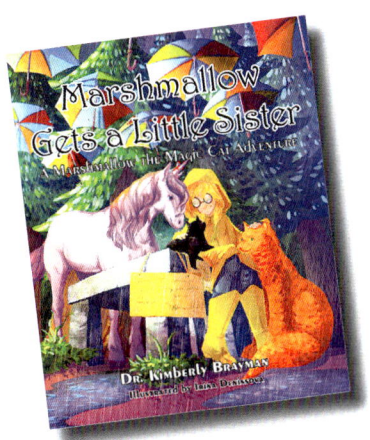

Check out the
new Sibley books on Amazon.

Made in United States
North Haven, CT
28 March 2022